Mother

A BOOK FOR MY

PAMELA WINTERBOURNE

PICTURES SELECTED BY WELLERAN POLTARNEES

LAUGHING ELEPHANT   MMIV

COPYRIGHT © 2003 BLUE LANTERN STUDIO

ISBN 1-883211-64-6

SECOND PRINTING ALL RIGHTS RESERVED PRINTED IN SINGAPORE

LAUGHING ELEPHANT BOOKS
3645 INTERLAKE AVENUE NORTH SEATTLE WASHINGTON 98103

www.LAUGHINGELEPHANT.com

Dear Mother

I send this book out of my love,
and in gratitude for the countless gifts
you have made to my life.

First of all you gave me your time,
the huge gifts of time a mother spends
watching, caring and loving.

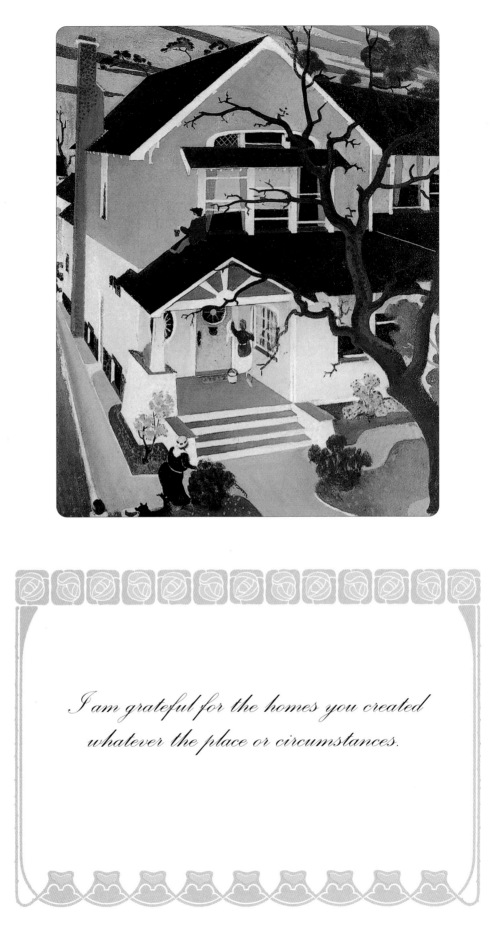

I am grateful for the homes you created
whatever the place or circumstances.

You gave me assurance of stability.
You were, and are, the one thing
I can count on in a shifting world.

Now I appreciate
all the worries that you silently carried.

When I was ill, or frightened,
you comforted me.

Thank you for all you taught me.

And encouraged me to learn.

I grew stronger
through your willingness to listen to me.

I am grateful
for the confidence you encouraged in me.

I will always remember
the stories you told me,
and the books you read to me.

You helped me to order life.

23

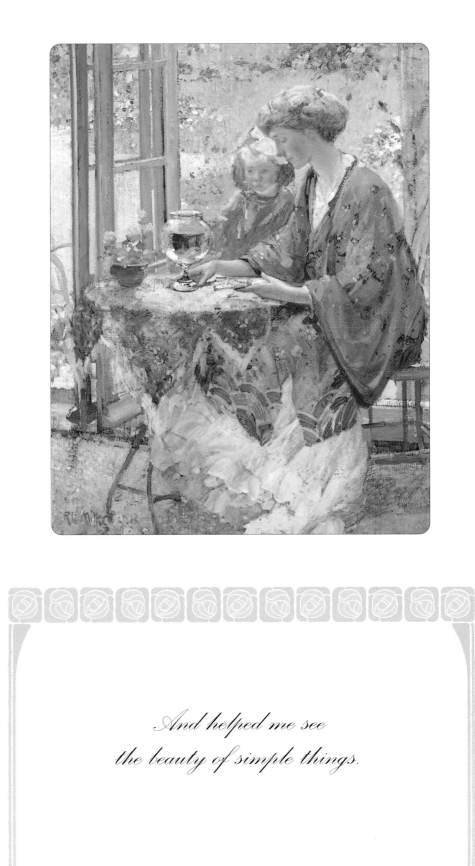

And helped me see
the beauty of simple things.

25

You encouraged me
to do things on my own,
but helped me when I needed help.

I thank you for your patience,

Your love

*And I will always remember
the many wonderful times
we have had together.*

Picture Credits

Cover   Jessie Willcox Smith. Magazine cover illustration, 1921.

Endpapers   Paolo Sala. "My Flowers," n.d.

Half-title   Florence J. and Margaret C. Hoopes. From *The New Day In and Day Out*, 1948.

Frontispiece   John White Alexander. "June," c. 1911.

Title Page   L. Hummel. From *Letty: A Study of a Child*, 1927.

2   André Hellé. From *Le Livre des Enfants*, c. 1920.

3   Elizabeth Nourse. "Meditation," 1902.

4   Preston Dickinson. "The World I Live In," 1920.

5   Edwin P. Couse. Magazine cover illustration, 1932.

6   James McNeill Whistler. "Mother and Child on a Couch," n.d.

7   Unknown. Magazine cover illustration, 1927.

8   Frederick Carl Frieseke. "Woman in Boudoir," 1914.

9   Frederick Carl Frieseke. "Portrait of a Girl (Pensive Model)," 1930.

10   Georges Lemmen. "Femme et enfant," 1907.

11   Florence Harrison. From *In The Fairy Ring*, 1908.

12   Johnny Gruelle. From *Little Sunny Stories*, 1919.

13   Walter Beach Humphrey. Magazine cover illustration, 1929.

14   Nadezhda Konstaninovic Kornienko. "In the Palace of Culture Ballet Class," 1956.

15   Augustus Edwin John. "The Sonnet," 1907.

16   Frank Desch. "Two Women Having Tea," n.d.

17   Laura Knight. "Two Girls on a Cliff," c. 1917.

18   Unknown. Magazine illustration, 1928.

19   Robert O. Reid. Illustration, c. 1932.

20   Margaret W. Tarrant. From *The Book of the Clock*, 1920.

21   Jessie Willcox Smith. Magazine cover illustration, 1921.

22   Frank B. Hoffman. Advertising illustration, 1928.

23   Christian Krohg. "A mother plaiting her little daughter's hair," 1883.

24   Richard Edward Miller. "Goldfish," 1912.

25   A.E. Marty. Magazine cover illustration, 1929.

26   Edward Potthast. "In the Surf," n.d.

27   Cheslie D'Andrea, Malcom Harvey and Marguerite Scott. From *Science for Work and Play*, 1959.

28   Mary Cassatt. "Mother Combing Sara's Hair," 1901.

29   Unknown. Advertising illustration, c. 1932.

30   Edith F. Butler. From *Stone's Silent Reading Book Two*, 1925.

31   Nicolai Fechin. "Mrs. Fechin and Her Daughter," 1922.

32   Helen M. Turner. "Lilies, Lanterns and Sunshine," 1923.

33   Henri-Joseph Lebasque. "Cueillant des Fleurs," 1923.

Back Cover   Norman Rockwell. Advertising illustration, 1922.